HOW PIPPI BEGAN

Karin replied, "Tell me about Pippi Long-stocking." It was a name she invented at that very moment.

Luckily, Astrid could do it. She began at once to make up a tale about a girl who lived alone and had no one to tell her what she had to do. A girl who was strong enough to lift a horse by herself. A girl who did not have to go to school if she did not want to. It was Karin who made up the name Pippi Longstocking, but it was her mother who gave Pippi her full name. It is Pippilotta Delicatessa Window-shade Mackrelmint Efraim's Daughter Long-stocking.

Karin Lindgren loved the stories about Pippi. Even after she got well, her mother continued to amuse her with more adventures of that wonderful girl.

Astrid Lindgren

Storyteller
to the World

JOHANNA HURWITZ
illustrated by Michael Dooling

PUFFIN BOOKS

PUFFIN BOOKS
An imprint of Penguin Random House LLC
375 Hudson Street
New York, New York 10014

First published in the United States of America by Viking Penguin,
a division of Penguin Books USA Inc., 1989
Published by Puffin Books, an imprint of Penguin Random House LLC, 2016

THE LIBRARY OF CONGRESS HAS CATALOGED THE VIKING PENGUIN EDITION AS FOLLOWS:
Hurwitz, Johanna. Astrid Lindgren: storyteller to the world / Johanna Hurwitz ;
illustrations by Michael Dooling.   p. cm.—(Women of our time)
Summary: Examines the life of the Swedish storyteller who created the well-known
Pippi Longstocking for her sick daughter and saw the story go on to be published
in fifty languages.
ISBN 978-0-670-82207-2 (hc)
1.Lindgren, Astrid, 1907– —Juvenile literature.
2. Authors, Swedish—20th century—Biography—Juvenile literature.
[1. Lindgren, Astrid, 1907– . 2. Authors, Swedish.]
I. Dooling, Michael, ill. II. Title. III. Series.
PT9875.L598Z69 1989 839.7'372—dc20 [b] 89-33913

Puffin Books ISBN 978-0-14-751668-8

Printed in the United States of America

1 3 5 7 9 10 8 6 4 2

The author would like to thank the Swedish Institute in Stockholm, Cecilia Ostlund of the Swedish Institute for Children's Books, and Kerstin Kvint for their assistance. Also, special thanks to Ingrid Kirna for her translations from the Swedish.

CONTENTS

CONTENTS

one

A SWEDISH CHILDHOOD

In the early years of last century, four children lived with their parents on a farm in Sweden. The children were named Gunnar, Astrid, Stina, and Ingegerd. Gunnar was the oldest and he was a boy. The others were his sisters.

The children did not own fancy toys. There was no television and not even a radio. Their parents did not have a car or a telephone. Such inventions were very new and cost much money. They would not be found in the home of simple farm folk like Hannah and Samuel August Ericsson and their family.

Yet despite all these things that were missing from their lives, the children felt very rich. They had plenty of land on which to run and explore, a river in which to splash and swim, farm animals to pet and love, barns in which to play, and corners in which to hide.

"I cannot imagine any children having more fun than we had," Astrid, the oldest sister, said.

Astrid Anna Emilia Ericsson was born on November 14, 1907. The farm where she was raised was called Nas. It had been built 500 years before as a home for a minister. The house was painted red. All around it were apple trees. Astrid's great-grandfather and grandfather had lived here and worked this same land. Now her father was the farmer at Nas. In time, Astrid's brother, Gunnar, was expected to work here, too. Although the family lived on land owned by the church, the men were not ministers. They were humble farmers who rented the land from the church, generation after generation.

Nas was near the little town of Vimmerby, in the southeastern part of Sweden. Instead of having dirt roads, Vimmerby was big enough to have streets paved with cobblestones. On the last Wednesday of every month, vegetables and animals were sold outdoors on the streets of Vimmerby. People came from miles away to shop at the open-air market. They could buy carrots and cabbages, cows and pigs. But Astrid and her brother and sisters were mostly interested in the homemade candies that were for sale. The streets were crowded with shoppers. The Ericsson children had to push and shove to make a purchase with their pennies.

Astrid stared, with her blue eyes, at the city people who came to buy at the market. They seemed rich and snobbish to her. She was curious about their lives, which were so different from her own.

Every Sunday, dressed in their best clothes,

the family went to church. Good behavior was very important. Often, Astrid could not understand what the minister was talking about. However, when she asked her brother, Gunnar, if he could follow the sermon, she felt better. Gunnar said, "No I don't understand. But believe me, nobody else does either." So Astrid sat quietly. Instead of worrying about the minister's message, she thought her own thoughts.

Astrid and all the children believed that if you were bad, the devil would come and take you away. They had heard one of the cowmen on the farm telling stories about the devil. He told them that if you went to the cemetery where the dead were buried and walked around and around 12 times at midnight, you would see the devil in person. It was a scary thought, but it was also exciting. So one fall evening when she was about 10 years old, Astrid and her sister Stina (say "STEEN-a") secretly set out together to go to the cemetery.

They wanted to see if they would really meet the devil.

They went around the graveyard again and again, keeping count. At last they completed 12 circles, but the devil did not appear. However, it was only 9:00 at night. "We were not allowed to stay out any longer, therefore the devil never showed up," Astrid said.

Sweden is the largest of the countries in northern Europe known as Scandinavia. The others are Denmark, Norway, Finland, and Iceland. The Scandinavian people share a long history dating back hundreds of years. The Vikings were among the early Scandinavians and they were great seamen. They traveled to many other parts of the world. Some people believe that in the 10th century, long before the time of Columbus, one of these Viking explorers, Leif Ericson, discovered America.

Swedish winters are long and hard. There is much snow, which is delightful for children to play in. But the snow makes life difficult for farmers with livestock to care for. The sun rises late in the morning and sets soon after 3 in the afternoon.

On the other hand, during the summer, the sun can be seen late into the night. This is known as "the midnight sun." It occurs in the more northern parts of Sweden. There the light is bright enough that one can read a book out of doors at midnight!

Whatever the outside temperature, Astrid and her brother and sisters lived in a home filled with the warmth of love and affection. Astrid knew that her father had fallen in love with her mother when he was only 13 years old and his wife-to-be was only 9. "The unusual thing was that my father, most unlike all other farmers I have met, every day told her his love so wonderfully," Astrid has recalled.

The children had the security of two loving parents who "were there all the time if we needed them," she said. "If we did not need them, they left us free to roam around Nas."

The Ericsson children played and worked hard. It was wonderful for Astrid to have a brother just 1 year older and her sister, Stina, only 3 years younger. Astrid always had playmates to join in the games she invented. Gunnar, too, could think of clever things to do. Once he took a chicken egg and put it in an owl's nest. It hatched there, to the great surprise of the mama owl! Years later, when she was writing her book *The Children of Noisy Village*, Astrid remembered what her brother had done and had one of the boys in the story do the same thing.

"We played and played and played, and it is a wonder we didn't play ourselves to death," Astrid recalled as an adult. "We were climbing like apes in trees and on roofs; we jumped from lumber piles and haylofts so that our innards complained; we crawled through our dangerous tunnels in the sawdust heap; we were swimming in the river long before we knew how to swim." The children did not pay any attention to their mother's rule not to go deeper in the water than their belly buttons. "But all four of us survived," Astrid marveled.

The children were trained to behave "with order and the fear of God, but in our playful life we were wonderfully free and never controlled."

From a very young age, the Ericsson children had their own jobs around the farm. Some of the work was boring and hard. At the age of 6, Astrid would bend over in the fields to thin out the growing vegetables, as the sun beat down on her blond braids. She cut prickly nettles to feed the chickens. Other jobs were more fun. One of Astrid's chores was to bring coffee to the farm workers in the fields. Then, as the men took their coffee break, she would sit and listen to them speak. They gossiped about local matters. They also talked of politics and the big war that was being fought just then in Europe. It was the time of World War I. Although Sweden did not fight in the war, everyone knew and talked about it.

Taking care of her baby sister Ingegerd

("IN-ge-yard") was another one of Astrid's chores. Often it was her job to put the little girl to sleep. Astrid discovered that she could do two things at once. She loved reading. It was possible for her to read her latest book

and sing the story aloud to the baby. In that way, she could amuse herself and also succeed in making Ingegerd fall asleep.

More than any of the others in her family, Astrid loved stories and books. Their home life was rich in so many areas, but it did not provide her with books. Luckily, however, there was a cowman who worked for Astrid's father. The cowman's daughter, Edith, introduced Astrid to the world of fairy tales. They used to sit in the kitchen where Edith lived and read aloud all the wonderful stories.

There were no public libraries, and books for young children were not found in many bookstores in those days. Astrid's first book, all her own to keep, was *Snow White*. One of the teachers Astrid had in kindergarten or first grade came up with a grand idea. Every year at Christmas time, the teacher took around a catalog of children's books and magazines. Each child could order one as a holiday present.

Years later, Astrid Lindgren could still remember how those books smelled. It was a special smell all its own, different from everything else in the world. She thought nothing could compare to the wonderful smell of a book!

As she grew older, Astrid read *Robinson Crusoe, Tom Sawyer,* and *Huckleberry Finn.* Often she would act out the stories, with her brother and sisters all becoming characters from the books. For one whole summer, the children acted out scenes from one of Astrid's favorite books, *Anne of Green Gables.*

In addition to her immediate family, there were many other people who were important in Astrid's childhood. The young hired girls who worked in the kitchen were almost like part of her family. They lived in the house, too. The kitchen was an important part of the home, especially during the cold winter days. Astrid often listened to the hired girls speaking as they went about their chores of cooking and washing. They talked about their boyfriends and about life.

From time to time, there were large family gatherings. Then all the cousins had a chance to play together while their parents gossiped and caught up on news. Food, which was simple during the week, was much more fancy during such gatherings. To the children, it seemed as if they only sat at the table and ate and ate.

The dinner would begin with a traditional Swedish smorgasbord ("SMORE-gos-bord"), a buffet of smoked and pickled herring and other fish, cold meats, cheeses, hard-boiled eggs, pickles, breads, and other items. It was more than enough food to satisfy the children.

But when the smorgasbord was finished, the real meal of steak and vegetables began. Of course, there was dessert with coffee and cake. The children did not have room for all there was to eat. They were amazed that the adults could sit so long just eating, eating, eating. Then, when the meal finally ended, it was time to go home again.

They rode home wrapped in warm blankets in their father's carriage pulled by two horses. It was lovely riding together in the dark. If it was Christmas time, they huddled together to

keep warm and listened to the bells around the horses' necks. "It was nice to be born at that time," Astrid Lindgren recalled.

Yet when people asked her what she remembered most from her childhood, it was not the people or the celebrations, the meals or the monthly market. She remembered nature and its variety of smells. She could never forget the growing strawberries and blueberries, hills yellow with wildflowers, and the woods and meadows and streams. Years later, she could still smell those freshly blooming flowers and recall the feel and smell of a newborn chick in her hand. And she remembered the smells and sounds at milking time as the warm milk hit the pail. Those were the memories that lasted forever.

two

OFF TO STOCKHOLM

When Astrid was in her early teens, her school friends insisted that she would grow up to be a writer. After all, they knew how much she liked books. "You will be the Selma Lagerlof of Vimmerby," they said. They were thinking of the famous Swedish novelist who was the first woman to win the Nobel Prize for Literature. The Nobel Prize is an international award and the highest honor an author can receive.

Astrid disagreed. Just because she liked to

read books didn't mean that she would be able to write them. She felt strongly that it was much better never to write any book than to sit down and write a bad one. She remembered reading in the Bible that there is no end to the making of books. One thing Astrid thought she knew for sure: She would not add to the number of books that were around.

By the age of 19, Astrid had completed her education at the local school in Vimmerby. She decided to go to Stockholm, the capital of Sweden. Her plan was to study typing and the other skills she would need to become a secretary. Then she would be able to get a job and support herself.

It was hard for Astrid to get used to city life. Everything was so different from her days on the farm. She rented a small room with a bed and other simple furniture in the home of an elderly widow. Astrid's rent money also paid for her meals at the house. Two other young women rented rooms at the same house. The three housemates quickly agreed that the food was terrible. Day after day, they were given the same fish to eat because it was cheap.

Finally, one of the young women complained. "Why must we have this fish again today?" she wanted to know. "We ate it yesterday and we ate it the day before yesterday as well."

"I went to the market and they had such wonderful fish that I couldn't resist," the landlady said. The fish did not seem wonderful to Astrid or the other young women.

Often Astrid felt hungry. The portions she was served were so small. One evening, when the landlady was out, the three young women went into the kitchen. They looked for something to eat. They decided to make themselves sandwiches and hot chocolate. There was a gas stove in the kitchen. It was quite unlike the wood-burning stove that Astrid had known back home in Nas. Neither she nor the two others knew how to use this more modern

appliance. At last they managed to light the stove with a match.

They heated the milk for their drink. When it was ready, they tried to turn off the stove. They took turns turning the knobs on the stove. The flame grew bigger. Finally Astrid hit on the plan to blow out the flame.

Later that evening, the maid, who worked for Astrid's landlady, walked into a gas-filled kitchen. Luckily no one was harmed, and luckily, too, there was no explosion caused by the leaking gas.

Time passed and the distasteful, boring meals continued. Astrid looked back longingly on the pleasant meals at Nas. She had no money to move to another house. One day, the father of one of her housemates came to visit. The girl complained to her father about the terrible meals that were served.

"Why don't you give these girls some meat?" the father asked the landlady. "Why don't you make meatballs, for example."

"Meatballs are for gentlemen," the landlady explained.

The three girls were shocked that they were not considered worthy of meat. Fish was good enough for them! The angry father said that his daughter would move away if the food did not improve at once. In the end, a bit of meat was served to them, even if they weren't gentlemen.

In time, Astrid rented another room in another house. One day, she went out and left her key inside. The landlady returned home and she, too, had forgotten her key to the house. There was no way to get inside. However, the landlady noticed that a top-floor window had been left open. She asked Astrid to climb the stairs in the house next door and then to go out through a fifth floor window in the hallway and onto the roof. Trying hard not to look down, Astrid walked across the roof and onto the roof of the next building. Then she climbed through the open window and was able to open the door from the inside. It was an adventure like those that children would read about one day in her book *Mischievous Meg*.

Astrid spent as little money as possible and she worked hard. Nas was hundreds of miles away. It was too expensive and too long a trip for her to go home to visit. But she missed everyone and everything.

Astrid remembered the wonderful holidays she had celebrated with her family. In the past, the long dark and cold winter had always been brightened by the joyful Christmas celebrations. She thought back to the happy years when, on December 13, she had been dressed in a white robe with a crown of candles on her head. She walked carefully, so as not to upset the candles or spill anything. It was Saint Lucia Day and she had the special honor of bringing breakfast to all her family.

Sitting in her small rented room, Astrid remembered, too, all the preparations at Nas

for Christmas. The old farmhouse had been thoroughly cleaned and special foods were baked. There was gingerbread, cut into the shapes of farm animals. There were other holiday breads and cakes, too. The smell of the baking filled the house.

Then Astrid and Gunnar and Stina had decorated the rooms by cutting out paper stars and hanging them in the windows. And everywhere, there were candles to bring light to the dark season. The candles reminded everyone that after December 22, the darkest day of the year, the sun would return. Soon the nights would not be so very, very long.

In the spring, Astrid recalled the Easter celebrations. In the old days, it was believed that witches gathered on Good Friday. Fires were built on the night before Easter to scare them off. People danced around the bonfires, waiting for Easter sunrise before they went off to church. While no one at Nas still believed in witches, they still built a bonfire. But how could you do that in the middle of a big and modern city like Stockholm?

Astrid was used to having a big family around her. She missed her brother and sisters. She missed the friendly household helpers who had always seemed like part of her family, too. Without this warmth and love and activity around her, the days in Stockholm were a sad, lonely, and unhappy time for Astrid.

Still, years later, Astrid Lindgren said, "To be alone is best. There is no loneliness that frightens me. Deep down we all remain alone. Without loneliness and poetry I believe I could hardly survive." For despite her loneliness, Astrid grew stronger than ever before. Her love for literature kept her company. She learned to look within herself for comfort and companionship. Years later, she wrote about many children who were lonely. There is Eric, who is befriended by Karlsson-on-the-roof. There are also the heroes of *Mio, My Son* and *Rasmus and the Vagabond*. Most important of all is Pippi Longstocking, who lives alone but is not unhappy.

In time, Astrid learned how to do short-hand, a way of writing words quickly, using just a few lines in place of letters. She also became a fast typist. At last, she was able to get work as a secretary. Her first job was with a company that sold radios. In 1928, radios were still a new invention. But more and more people were buying them.

Astrid's next job turned out to be very important in her life. She was hired to work for the Royal Automobile Club. The company produced tour guides for car owners. One of Astrid's fellow workers was Sture Lindgren. Astrid did not guess that her coworker was to become her husband.

On April 4, 1931, the 23-year-old Astrid Ericsson became Astrid Lindgren. Soon the Lindgrens were the parents of a son named Lars. Their daughter, Karin, was born in 1934.

When asked what children need nowadays,

Astrid Lindgren joked, "Kids need to select their parents very carefully." She herself was "not a mother who sat in the park like other mothers," her son, Lars, recalled. Instead, the slim, active mother climbed the trees along with the children. She liked to play, too, and didn't want to be left out. "She had as much fun as we did," said Lars.

She enjoyed staying home with Karin and Lars and watching them grow. "That our Lord let children be children before they grew up was one of His better ideas," she says. As her children grew older, she amused them with stories that she made up. Stories from their mother were a special treat for Lars and Karin.

From time to time, however, Astrid would get a job as a secretary. This would take her out of the house for just one or two days. It kept her shorthand and typing skills fresh. Astrid had worked hard to learn them and she didn't want to forget them. Maybe such talents would be useful in the future.

In the late 1930s, all of Europe knew that another big war was coming. Germany began to conquer the nearby countries. During this tense time, Astrid kept a diary. She wrote about all that was happening in Europe.

In the summer of 1940, Astrid was offered a secret government job. It was work she could do at home. She was to open letters and read them carefully. She checked that there was no information in the letters that would help the Germans. As in the last war, Sweden did not fight in World War II. But Astrid's job was so secret that she didn't even write about it in her diary. Still, diary writing was a regular part of Astrid's life. It was only a matter of time until she began writing stories, too.

three

THE BIRTH OF PIPPI LONGSTOCKING

Two unhappy events brought about the creation of Astrid Lindgren's most famous book for children, *Pippi Longstocking*. The first bad thing was in 1941. Seven-year-old Karin Lindgren became ill with pneumonia. She had to stay in the house and in bed.

Every evening, to entertain her daughter, Astrid told her a story. One evening, when she had run out of new ideas, Astrid said, "What should I tell you tonight?"

Karin replied, "Tell me about Pippi Long-stocking." It was a name she invented at that very moment.

Luckily, Astrid could do it. She began at once to make up a tale about a girl who was as unusual as her name. A girl who lived alone and had no one to tell her what she had to do. A girl who was strong enough to lift a horse by herself. A girl who did not have to go to school if she did not want to. It was Karin who made up the name Pippi Longstocking, but it was her mother who gave Pippi her full name. It is Pippilotta Delicatessa Windowshade Mackrel-mint Efraim's Daughter Longstocking.

Karin Lindgren loved the stories about Pippi. Even after she got well, her mother continued to amuse her with more adventures of that wonderful girl.

The second piece of bad luck that brought about the creation of *Pippi Longstocking* took place three years later, in March of 1944. This time it was Astrid herself who was in bed. She had slipped and fallen as she walked on the icy, snow-covered streets of Stockholm. With a sprained ankle, Astrid found herself unable to walk around, even in the house. She needed something to do to pass the time. Astrid decided to write down the Pippi stories that she had been telling and retelling to Karin.

In May of 1944, Karin would celebrate her 10th birthday. Astrid decided that if she wrote out the Pippi tales, she could present them as a special gift to her daughter. Once the stories were written, however, another plan occurred to Astrid. She decided to send a copy of the stories to a children's book publisher.

She did not really think that the stories would be published as a book. In fact, she found herself a bit upset with Pippi. She wrote a letter that she mailed together with her story. It ended with the words, "In the hope you won't notify the Child Welfare Committee." After all, 9-year-old Pippi lived alone. She didn't go to school or obey rules. Astrid had two children of her own. Perhaps people would think that a woman who wrote such a story was not a good mother.

Sure enough, the typed pages of the Pippi story were returned. The publisher was not going to make it into a book. Even so, Astrid's writing career was about to begin that year. She learned that the publishing house of Raben and Sjogren was having a contest for books written about girls. Interested in trying her luck, Astrid wrote another story. In the fall of 1944, Astrid learned that her story *The Confidences of Britt-Mari* won second prize in the contest. It was one of the proudest moments of her life.

The Confidences of Britt-Mari was written in the form of a diary. Britt-Mari is a proper, well-behaved girl, quite different from Pippi Longstocking. Such a girl is not as interesting a subject for a story. Perhaps that is the reason the book has never been translated from Swedish into English.

With one success behind her, Astrid was eager to try again. When the same publishing company held another contest the following year, Astrid found the pages of the Pippi story that she had put away. She mailed them to the judges.

Pippi Longstocking did not win second prize. It was the first prize winner for 1945!

Soon after, *Pippi Longstocking* was published by Raben and Sjogren. Swedish girls, and boys, too, agreed with Karin Lindgren and the publishers that this was a heroine that they loved. Pippi was very different from the girls they had met in children's books before. She was not quiet or sweet or gentle. Instead she was naughty and loud, strong and brave.

Some of the early reviewers in Sweden could not accept this type of behavior. Articles were written about the bad taste of the Raben and Sjogren judges to select such a book for an award. And there were even letters to the editor published in the newspaper complaining about Pippi's terrible manners.

Still, children loved Pippi. And that meant bookstores sold many, many copies of the book. It was not long before publishers in other countries began to bring out translations of the story in their languages, too. In time, *Pippi Longstocking* would be translated into more than 50 languages. Astrid Lindgren would become the most translated of all Swedish writers. Even Selma Lagerlof, the Nobel Prize winner, has not been translated into so many languages. *Pippi Longstocking* is one of the twelve most translated books in the world today. That means that almost everywhere children know her name—or some form of it.

The name that Karin made up for her mother one evening in 1941 was "Pippi Langstrump," which is the Swedish title of the book. Other names that Pippi has in other countries include:

Bibi Meia-longa	in Portugal
Mademoiselle Brindacier	in France
Peppi Pitkatossu	in Finland

Pippi Calzelunghe	in Italy
Nagakutsushita-No-Pippi	in Japan
Peppi Dlinnyjculok	in Russia
Pipi Duga Carapa	in Yugoslavia
Fizia Ponczoszanka	in Poland
Pippi Langkous	in Holland
Lina Langsokkur	in Iceland
Bilbee Bat-Gerev	in Israel
Pipi Gurab-baland	in Iran

In every language, Pippi Longstocking is 9 years old. She has hair the color of a carrot, which she wears in two tight braids that stick out. Her potato-shaped nose is covered with freckles. Pippi always wears a black stocking on one leg and a brown one on the other. And on her feet, she wears shoes that are twice as large as they should be. Pippi lives alone because her mother is dead and her father, who was a sea captain, has been lost at sea. However, even though she is an orphan, Pippi is happy. She knows that her mother is an angel up in heaven. She feels just as sure that her father is alive on a cannibal island where he has been made king.

With a suitcase filled with gold pieces to pay for all her needs, and no one to tell her what to do, Pippi leads a grand life. Since she is strong enough to lift a horse or to overpower a policeman, she does not have to be afraid of anything. And she is never lonely. She makes friends with Tommy and Annika, who live right next door. Best of all, she has her own horse and a monkey named Mr. Nilsson. What more could any child want?

Pippi stands for every child's dream of doing exactly what he or she wants without an adult saying no. She has the bravery and the daring that all children wish for. When they read her story, they too, at least for a short time, become Pippi Longstocking, with all her marvelous ways and adventures. And even when the book is completed, children carry the image of Pippi about with them in their heads. She is a great companion both on paper and in a child's imagination. No one has ever counted how many children dress up as Pippi Longstocking each year at costume parties or on Halloween!

Astrid began to receive letters from her readers. They all begged her to write more about this marvelous heroine. She wrote two more books: *Pippi Goes on Board* and *Pippi in the South Seas.*

In Sweden, Pippi has appeared in many other forms. Her story has been retold as a picture book for very young children, as a play to act out, as a comic strip, as easy readers for young students, as a coloring book, and as a songbook. Pippi's adventures have also been the basis for a TV series and for several motion pictures.

Pippi Longstocking did not reach the United States until 1950. A copy of the story was sent to The Viking Press, an American publishing company.

The editors at Viking decided to publish Pippi in English. There are many publishing companies in the United States. It amused the Scandinavian, Astrid Lindgren, that her book would be published by a company named for the early Scandinavians.

Instead of using the illustrations that were in the Swedish edition, new pictures were made by an American illustrator, Louis Glanzman. Although the early readers wrote good things about the book, the sales began slowly.

May Massee, the children's book editor at Viking, wrote to Astrid on March 30, 1951: "It does not look as though Pippi is going to have the enormous success she had in Sweden." No one could guess from those early sales that in time more than 5 million copies would be sold in the United States. And that number continues to grow!

The increasing sales of *Pippi Longstocking* and the piles of letters from eager readers made the American editors want to publish more books by Astrid Lindgren. In 1952, her book *Bill Bergson, Master Detective* was published in the United States. Soon her books were sold here regularly. Her readers awaited these new books impatiently.

Astrid Lindgren, who had once told her friends that she would never become a writer, seemed to have an endless supply of stories waiting to be recorded.

four

AUTHOR, EDITOR, TRANSLATOR

Astrid Lindgren's fame around the world is mostly due to her creation of Pippi Longstocking. However, she has written more than 40 other books as well. Although she didn't want to sprain her ankle again, Astrid discovered that she enjoyed the method she used in writing that first book about Pippi. It had worked so well before that she continued to use it. So almost always, when she was working on a new tale, she got back into bed, stretched out her legs, and began writing. Some stories were written in her bed in Stockholm. The others were written while resting on the balcony of her summer house on the Baltic Sea, about 30 miles from Stockholm.

Many books were written there "with one eye on the water and the ships passing and the other eye on my writing," she said. The movement of the ships certainly did not take her mind from her writing. Every year for more than 30 years, Astrid wrote at least one new book. And all the books were written and rewritten using the shorthand that she had learned when she trained to be a secretary.

Madicken is a book about a highly imaginative and naughty girl that was first published in Sweden in 1960. It appeared in the United States two years later with the title *Mischievous Meg*. The heroine is described as able to "get her wild ideas as fast as a pig can blink." It would certainly seem that as the creator of Meg and Pippi and all her other books, Astrid, too, got wild ideas as fast as a pig can blink!

There is a great variety in the types of stories that Astrid has written. In addition to the imaginative fantasy of Pippi, there are exciting detective stories about a young boy named Bill Bergson, and a lively series about the youngsters living in Noisy Village. Also, there are fairy tales, picture books, and career and travel books. The mood of some of the later books by Astrid Lindgren seems dark and serious when compared with the happy, light-hearted adventures of *Pippi Longstocking, Mischievous Meg,* or *Emil in the Soup Tureen.*

Books like *Mio, My Son,* as well as *Ronia, the Robber's Daughter* and *The Brothers Lionheart,* are concerned with the somber issues of good and evil and life and death. Yet in each of these stories, the reader finds the strong love between parent and child, and between brothers and sisters. This comes straight from Astrid's own happy childhood.

While the Pippi books were still new in the United States, Astrid wrote to her American editor, "My best books are about six children

in a little village, and I know in my heart that they are better than Pippi."

Called the Bullerby stories in Sweden, in English translation, these books became the stories about the children of Noisy Village. Bullerby is very, very similar to Vimmerby, the town of Astrid's childhood. The stories are filled with happy, carefree young children playing together, celebrating the changing seasons and the wonderful Swedish holidays and traditions.

One child wrote to Astrid to ask if Noisy Village really existed. "If it does," she said, "I don't want to live in Vienna any longer."

More than any of her other books, the stories of Noisy Village reflect Astrid's memories of her childhood. Britta, Anna, Olaf, Karl, Bill, and Lisa play the games that Astrid played with her brother and sisters. They climb the same trees and eat the same meals that Astrid has never forgotten.

Pippi Longstocking showed that Astrid could

write about a girl who had energy and imagination. She could write the same about a boy. A rascal named Emil who lives in Vimmerby is the hero of a series of books. Once again, Astrid has described the old customs she remembered from her childhood. The reader can almost taste the holiday dishes.

In a chapter in *Emil's Pranks*, she lists down a full page the foods that were served the day after Christmas as a special treat to the poor people of the town. They included:

A dish of black pudding
A dish of pork sausages
A dish of liver paste
A dish of headcheese
A dish of meatballs
A dish of veal cutlets
A dish of spareribs of pork
A dish of oatmeal sausages
A dish of potato sausages
A dish of salmagundi

A dish of salt beef
A dish of ox tongue
A huge ham
A dish of cheesecake
A plate of rye bread
A plate of syrup bread
A crate of juniper berry drinks
A can of milk
A bowl of rice pudding
A bowl of cream cheese
A dish of preserved plums
An apple pie
A jug of cream
A jug of strawberry juice
A jug of pear ginger
And a suckling pig garnished with sugar

Even children who cannot recognize all these dishes must lick their lips and imagine the feast.

"It is my childhood that I long to return to. . . . When I go home [to the farm outside

Vimmerby], I intensely experience my child-hood again and again. Everything I write has really taken its hue from my own experi-ence, perhaps not directly, but indirectly, like some kind of breeding ground from which the books grow," she has said.

One thing in Astrid's books that may be surprising to American readers is her use of names. Often a name in one book is repeated in another. Pippi's pet monkey is Mr. Nilsson. So it is startling to later meet the next-door neighbor of Mischievous Meg with the same name. And what about the farmer Nielson who offers to adopt the orphan boy Rasmus in *Rasmus and the Vagabond*? Using the same names over and over again seems strange from an author who has already proven her skill at cre-ating original names. Could it be that she had run out of new ideas?

The reason that the same names are used frequently in Astrid's books is that this is very common in Swedish life. Many people of Swedish background have names like Anderson, Ericsson, or some other name ending with *son*. That is because, long ago, people did not have last names. Children were given their own first name. Then their father's name was added on to show to which family they belonged.

Other Swedish family names grew out of the places where people lived. *Dahl* means valley, *berg* means mountain, *strand* means by the shore, *stad* means in a city, and *gren* means by a fork in the road. As a result of these methods of giving last names, many names are often repeated in Sweden. In order to avoid confusion, the telephone book identifies people by listing their jobs along with their names. A million and a half people live in Stockholm. There are about 1,800 listings for the name Lindgren. Apparently, many people named Lind once lived near a fork in the road. The Stockholm phone book even listed a total of eleven women named Astrid Lindgren. But not one of these was the author of *Pippi Longstocking.*

She had chosen to keep her privacy through an unlisted number.

Just as *Pippi Longstocking* was received with mixed reactions when it was published in 1945, another debate arose in Sweden when *The Brothers Lionheart* was published. This was almost 30 years later, in 1973. Some critics felt the book was not for children because it deals with the subjects of death and evil. But others thought so highly of the book that they urged that Astrid Lindgren be nominated for the Nobel Prize.

Years before the book was published, Astrid had said, "I don't think it's right to completely ignore death in literature for children. Many children feel real dread of death. . . . When I was little I thought we all died and then we met again in heaven. The only problem was that we wouldn't die at the same time."

Astrid's story is about two brothers who die and meet again in a faraway kingdom. How they bravely fight against evil is both exciting and moving. Best of all, for many children, it has calmed their fears. Many children have written to Astrid saying, "Now I'm not afraid of death anymore."

Astrid Lindgren's contribution to Swedish children's literature is not just through the books she has written. She also had another and very important role.

Astrid had won prizes three years in a row in the Raben and Sjogren contest. Then one of the judges suggested to the book publishing company that they would be smart to offer Astrid a job. So beginning in 1946, Astrid wrote her own stories at home each morning and spent every afternoon working at the publisher's offices.

It was a good arrangement. She would earn a regular salary even if there were no book sales. This was very important, because Sture Lindgren became ill in the late 1940s. Astrid helped to nurse her husband for several years. Sadly, in June of 1952, he died. By then, Lars was married and no longer living at home. But 44-year-old Astrid had to support herself and Karin.

One of Astrid's jobs as editor was to select American books that Swedish children would enjoy reading. Such popular books as *Homer Price*, by Robert McCloskey, and *Charlotte's Web*, by E. B. White, were translated and published by Raben and Sjogren. Astrid even did a small bit of translation herself. Several simple American picture books on the publisher's list were translated into Swedish by Anna Ericsson or Emilia Ericsson. Both names were Astrid's. She had made up pseudonyms ("SOO-do-nims"), or false names, by using her middle and maiden names. She translated Garth Williams's *Rabbits' Wedding* and several books by H. A. Rey, including *See the Circus* and *Where's My Baby?*

Among her own favorite books for children by other writers are the Moomin stories by the Finnish writer Tove Jansson. And *Winnie-the-*

Pooh, by A. A. Milne, is the book that Astrid Lindgren considers to be the greatest children's book of all time.

Astrid Lindgren worked at Raben and Sjogren for 24 years. When she began, the publisher was losing money and close to failing. However, the success of the books she wrote and those she selected to publish was very great. By 1970, when Astrid retired as an editor, Raben and Sjogren was Sweden's biggest publisher of books for children.

five

ASTRID LINDGREN AND THE WORLD

In 1907, the year that Astrid Lindgren was born, an important book was published for Swedish children. The book was *The Wonderful Adventures of Nils* by Selma Lagerlof. She wrote of a naughty boy who becomes an elf and flies on the back of a goose over the Swedish countryside. Written to be used as a geography text, the book is also an exciting fantasy. It has become a children's classic, not just in Sweden, but all over the world.

In 1950, the Swedish Library Association

created an award called the Nils Holgersson Plaque. It honors the finest Swedish children's book of the year. It is similar to the Newbery Medal, which is awarded in the United States.

It was chance that Astrid and the fictional Nils Hogersson were "born" the same year. But it was talent, not chance, that made her the first person to receive this new Swedish award. The same Astrid Lindgren who, as a young girl, had fiercely denied to her friends that she would become the Selma Lagerlof of Vimmerby.

In 1958, Astrid received the Hans Christian Andersen Medal. The medal is named after the 19th-century Danish writer of such fairy tales as *The Princess and the Pea* and *The Ugly Duckling*. The Hans Christian Andersen Medal is an international award and the highest honor that can be given to a writer of children's books.

Astrid Lindgren's fame was no longer limited to the Swedish borders, nor to Europe either. In fact, she became so well known in the United States that in August of 1960, she wrote to her American editor, Annis Duff, saying, "*Who's Who in America* has offered me a copy of the book since they included me in it. . . . Perhaps they do not know I am a foreigner." Sure enough, the Swedish writer was listed in volume 32 of this book of short biographies of famous Americans. Pippi's creator not American? She belongs to the world!

In 1978, Astrid received the Peace Prize of the German Book Trade. This is the highest honor it can give a writer. They said she "was an author who delicately, yet persistently, teaches tolerance, fairness, understanding and responsibility." No other author of children's books has ever received this award.

The year 1978 was a busy one, with many more awards and honorary degrees. Writing to her American editor, Astrid mentioned the honors she was receiving. She wrote, "I don't tell this in order to boast, just to let you know how scared I am (at having to deliver so many acceptance speeches) and how it prevents me from what I would really like—to write a new children's book. So I have decided: Next year I will do nothing but WRITE. It is the most important thing for me. So I think I had better put a sign on my door: No awards accepted! Do you think I am ungrateful? No I am not. I am just tired."

At the same time that Astrid's books were winning awards for her, still another honor was attached to her name. An award named after her was established by the International Federation of Translators. First presented in 1981 and called the Astrid Lindgren Translation Prize, it is given every three or four years to honor a children's book translation.

In the spring of 1987, the Swedish government found still another way to honor Astrid. A series of ten postage stamps was put on sale. Each stamp had a drawing of one of the characters from her books.

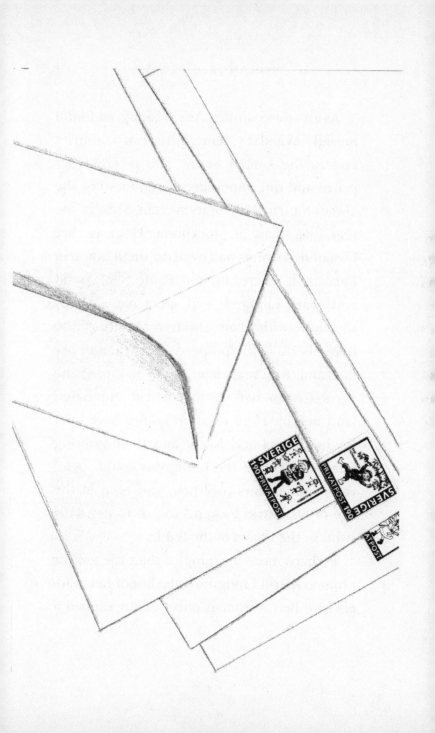

As an award winner, Astrid Lindgren found herself invited to many European countries and to the United States. She received her prizes and did some sightseeing, too. But she always returned home to Sweden. Most of the year, she spent in Stockholm. However, her husband's parents had owned a small house in Furusund. There, on the Baltic Sea, Astrid and Sture Lindgren had spent many happy vacations with their children. In time, the house became the property of Astrid and her husband. And years later, with the money she earned from her writing, Astrid purchased land nearby. Here vacation homes were built for both Lars and Karin and their growing families. Now all the Lindgrens could spend the summer days together. And even at the age of 80, Astrid looked forward to her daily swim in the waters of the Baltic.

Perhaps more meaningful than the awards given to Astrid Lindgren is the honor her readers give her. A woman once silently slipped a piece of paper into Astrid's hand. "Thank you for brightening up a gloomy childhood," she had written on the paper. "If I've succeeded in brightening up just one gloomy childhood, I'm satisfied," Astrid has said.

One year, a letter arrived at the offices of The Viking Press from an 11-year-old girl in St. Louis, Missouri. She asked if she could list her Shetland sheepdog with the American Kennel Club under the name Pippi Longstocking. The dog had long white stockings on her front paws and black coloring on the rest of her body. Pippi Longstocking seemed the perfect name. Permission was granted! And it is quite likely that over the years many other dogs, as well as cats and ponies, too, have been named Pippi Longstocking—even if their owners never took the time to write the author or the publisher.

For years, Astrid had used her writing talents and her name to fight for animal rights. Since her childhood on the farm at Nas, she had loved animals. It angered her to know that modern animals were fed drugs, made to live in cramped spaces, and unable to graze out in the fields, under the sun. Because she was upset that they were killed in a cruel manner, she no longer ate chicken.

Astrid wrote several stories about better care of animals. These stories were printed in Swedish newspapers. "Every pig is entitled to a happy pig life," she wrote.

Because her name is so well known in Sweden, political leaders read her stories and could not ignore what she said. It was not the first time she had written for adult readers. In 1976, she wrote a story to complain about the high tax rate in Sweden. Her tale of a person forced to beg because high taxes had taken all his money influenced the voters. That year, the ruling political party was defeated in the election. Astrid Lindgren was credited with its downfall. She was also credited with bringing lower taxes to Sweden.

On November 14, 1987, Astrid celebrated

her 80th birthday. The prime minister of Sweden went to visit her. The American and Soviet ambassadors brought their good wishes, too.

The prime minister gave her a very special gift on her birthday. He told her that a new law would be put into effect within a few months. In the future, cows, pigs, and chickens would be treated better during their lives. And they would be killed in a less cruel manner. Animal lovers around the world rejoiced at this new Swedish policy. They hoped that Astrid Lindgren's birthday present would someday mean a better life for all animals.

The author of so many stories lived long enough to see her own life become a glorious tale. Like the people she stared at in the Vimmerby market so many years ago, she, too, became a rich city person. (But she was never a snob, as such people once seemed to her.) Today, many of the streets of Vimmerby are named after books by Astrid Lindgren. She owned the farm where she was raised. Although

none of the Ericsson family lives there today, the house would remain in the family. It was where family gatherings and celebrations took place.

Astrid Lindgren became both a grand-mother and a great-grandmother several times over. She was not a typical mother and she was not a typical grandmother either. Unlike most people, she never grew too old to play.

Despite her wonderful imagination, the lit-tle Swedish farm girl who played in the hay-lofts with her brother and sisters and made up fantastic stories to entertain them could never have dreamed that one day her stories would become so famous in Sweden and throughout the world.

With her books available in every modern language in the world, there is always a place on the globe where it is daytime. There is always a place where children are reading the books of Astrid Lindgren.

In the summer of 1988, I traveled to Sweden to meet Astrid Lindgren in person. Before our meeting, I went into a bookstore where shelves and shelves of her books were displayed in many languages.

In my hotel room, I turned on the radio to hear the Swedish language. I found a program on which a woman was obviously reading aloud. She spoke slowly and I could make out where one of those strange words ended and a new word began. The single word I recognized was the name Rasmus. What I could not guess, until I met her, was that I was listening to Astrid Lindgren reading from one of her books.

When I went to mail postcards to my friends back home, I discovered the postage stamps honoring the author. So even before I met her, I had heard her voice and seen ample evidence of her fame. But the best thing was meeting Astrid Lindgren in person. In her 80s, she has retained her vitality and humor.

Yet everyone who has read one of her books has met Astrid and listened to her voice, too. How lucky we are that one winter day she broke her ankle and launched her writing career.

J. H.

TIMELINE / INDEX